Copy our yoga poses as you follow us through
the alphabet, or just pretend you're one of the animals.
Don't worry if you can't get it exactly right —
enjoy yourself and be one with nature!

Armadillo

Armadillo curls up quick—
Stretch with us
To learn this trick!

Butterfly

Who's that fluttering by?
Join your hands and feet,
And smile at the butterfly.

Crocodile

Crocodile lives by the shore,
Plank with us and
Find out more!

Dog

Woof woof, let's get outdoors!
Like doggy and me—
Face down on all fours.

Elephant

Elephant likes a cool drink.
Bend down forward and
Let your head sink.

Fox

Little red fox in the wood,
Stretch your back and
You'll feel good!

Grasshopper

Grasshopper rarely sits still.
Let's all squat down
To help him chill.

Hippo

Dozing cool in the lake,
The giant hippo
Takes a break.

Iguana

Iguana green and bright—
Lunge with us
To your delight.

Jellyfish

Jellyfish wobbles by,
Lie on your back—
Look at the sky.

Koala

Koala hugs a leafy tree.
Twist your arms and legs,
And do it like me.

Lion

I'm a lion—hear me roar,
Sit like me and
Stretch some more!

Moon

Crescent moon in the sky,
Bend like me —
Watch clouds float by.

Nest

Two eggs in a nest,
I make a bow
And take a rest.

Owl

Hooty owl in the trees,
Look straight ahead,
Sit on your knees.

Like a piggy on the ground,
Touch your toes,
Roll all around.

Quack

See the dancing duck?
Stand on one leg
And make a quack!

Rainbow

Like these two friends,
Join your feet, join your hands,
Make a rainbow with two ends.

Shark

Speedy shark swims in the sea,
Do this pose
Like him and me.

Tiger

Get down on your paws—
See the stripey tiger,
With tail and claws?

Unicorn

Unicorn says hello,
Up on two legs,
Ready to go!

Volcano

Like the volcano I stand,
Arms and legs spread wide,
High up on black sand.

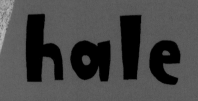 **hale**

Watch the whale in the sea,
Make a bridge,
Let's count to three.

X-ray fish

Flat like the X-ray fish,
I flap my hands
And go swosh-swish!

Yak

Strut like the hairy Yak,
Through hills and fields,
Then arch your back.

Rest with us for a while,
Enjoy the peace
And you will smile.

what is YOGA?

Yoga is an ancient tradition from India. The word *yoga* means "union" because it brings your body, your mind, and your spirit together.

The postures in yoga were developed by looking closely at nature and the animals living in it. This is why, in yoga, you can roar like a lion or stretch like a cat!

By practicing yoga regularly, you will get stronger, more balanced, and more flexible. Yoga can also help you concentrate and channel your energy.

Armadillo
Extended child's pose

Butterfly
Cobbler pose

Crocodile
Plank pose

Dog
Down-facing dog pose

Elephant
Standing forward bend

Fox
Three-legged dog pose

Grasshopper
Squat pose

Hippo
Child's pose

Iguana
Forward lunge

Jellyfish
Lying forward bend

Koala
Eagle pose

Lion
Lion pose

Moon
Crescent moon pose

Nest
Bow pose

Owl
Hero pose

Pig
Happy baby pose

Quack
Dancer's pose

Rainbow
Rainbow pose

Shark
Full locust pose

Tiger
Cat pose

Unicorn
Chair pose

Volcano
X pose

Whale
Bridge pose

X-ray fish
Locust pose

Yak
Cow pose

Zzzz
Sleeping pose

Brimming with creative inspiration, how-to projects, and useful information to enrich your everyday life, quarto.com is a favorite destination for those pursuing their interests and passions.

First published in 2016 by Walter Foster Jr., an imprint of The Quarto Group.
100 Cummings Center, Suite 265D, Beverly, MA 01915, USA.
T (978) 282-9590 **F** (978) 283-2742 **www.quarto.com • www.walterfoster.com**

Walter Foster Jr. titles are also available at discount for retail, wholesale, promotional, and bulk purchase. For details, contact the Special Sales Manager by email at specialsales@quarto.com or by mail at The Quarto Group, Attn: Special Sales Manager, 100 Cummings Center, Suite 265D, Beverly, MA 01915, USA.

ISBN: 978-1-60058-984-3

Digital edition published in 2016
eISBN: 978-1-63322-249-6

Printed in China
10 9 8 7 6 5 4 3 2

For Josie